Allow Your Soul To Lead

Volume 4

The Soul & The Human Aspect: A Love Story

A Channeled Text
Healing Series

Cindy Edison

Allow Your Soul to Lead: Volume 4
The Soul & The Human Aspect: A Love Story
Copyright © 2019 Cindy Edison
ISBN: 978-1796826418

All Rights Reserved. No part of this book may be reproduced, scanned or transmitted in any forms, digital, audio or printed, without the expressed written consent of the author.

The information contained in this book are the views of the author based on their experiences and opinions. Your results may differ.

Although the author and publisher have made every effort to ensure the information in this book was correct at press time, the author and publisher do not assume and hereby disclaim any liability to any party for any loss, damage, or disruption caused by errors or omissions, whether such errors or omissions result from negligence, accident, or any other cause.

Table Of Contents:

WELCOME	1
PRELUDE TO THE WORK	3
SOUL LOVE	7
WHAT'S LOVE GOT TO DO WITH IT?	9
OUR HUMAN ASPECT	17
THE ONENESS OF THE SOUL AND THE HUMAN ASPECT	19
HOW THE HUMAN ASPECT WAS CREATED	23
THE INHERENT LOVE OF THE HUMAN ASPECT FOR ITS SOUL ASPECT	27
YOUR SOUL IS THE EXPANDED VERSION OF YOU, ITS HUMAN ASPECT	31
THE SOUL'S LOVE FOR THE HUMAN ASPECT, EXTENDED THROUGH ITS EGO ASPECT	35
HOW THE HUMAN ASPECT FITS INTO THE PROCESS OF EVOLUTION	39
ALIGNMENT	43
OUR PARTING WORDS	47
QUOTES & COMMENTARY BY JOSEF	49

WELCOME

Greetings Dear One,

If you've taken it upon yourself to have read Volumes 1, 2 and 3, we believe you are getting our point and you can see where we are leading you which is back to love.

As we've discussed, this healing series will serve many purposes and our overall intention is to create a space, a vibrational space, that is for healing. This involves the alignment of the human aspect. When you are in alignment with your Soul, you are in the space of creation where all 'love' occurs which includes all healing. This is the vibrational space where no darkness resides; it is the pure and plain Truth of God as some of you refer to 'him'.

If you've read to this point, you understand our 'version' of God to be a pure vibration that is within all and vibrationally available to all as well, for this God is the true essence of who you really are and our intention for healing will deliver you, on our silver platter, back to the fullness and truth of You.

This volume will lay out the relationship between the Soul and the human aspect. For example, it will lay out the relationship between Us and Cindy, her Soul and her as our human aspect. She has agreed, prior to our beginning this project, to allow her own life experience to assist in these teachings. A brave one she is, by your human standards.

We will discuss and delve further into the true meaning of Love and all the ways in which the human aspect can experience it but the experience, if you allow it, will be from a different perspective which is the perspective of your Soul. Until now, the experience of Love has been more so taught than experienced, and as we move through this portion of our text, you will understand more of what that statement means.

The Soul & The Human Aspect

As we've said, along with and 'as' our dear friends Abraham, words do not teach. Experience is the true-life teacher and that is the track we will take in this Volume through the use of examples and opportunities to experience Love in a different way through visualization and communication with your own Soul. Cindy is demonstrating for you now, although you cannot 'see' her, communication with her Soul by typing as she receives words and blocks of thought. This is simply another language, although we would not call it foreign, for it is the most natural language the human aspect has ever been exposed to. It is unfortunate that this language has 'fallen by the wayside' so to speak, however that is part of our intention as well, which is to re-introduce you to the parts of yourself that have been lying dormant within you. Vibration is the language of the Soul and when you reacquaint yourself with it, you will experience it as you have when hopping on your bike after twenty years. It all comes back to you and this will too.

Our intention in bringing this message of the Soul to you at this time is important if we are all to create the New Earth in a physical plane. In order to manifest the New Earth where physical beings walk the earth as their Soul, the collective vibration must come first, for all manifestations begin with the thought and the thought manifests into a vibration, the vibration is matched by the Universe and physical manifestation occurs. This will happen one human aspect at a time.

Again, we thank you for your focus and attention to your own well-being which expands to the well-being of all of humanity as we forge ahead, taking our next step toward the collective New Earth vibration

We are Josef.

PRELUDE TO THE WORK

In this Volume, we will continue with the Love subject and how the Soul and the Human Aspect relate - or were meant to relate - to each other as the One. This is an important teaching because there is nothing more powerful than a human aspect who is in alignment with their Soul. As Abraham teaches, 'One in alignment is more powerful than a million who are not." This is not a statement to sneeze at for when you are in alignment with the Soul of you, the God-ness within you, you have the ability to do all things. This is where the creation energy stands in wait for alignment. It is where worlds are birthed and babies are conceived; it is where only well-being flows and it is where you create the reality you desire vibrationally.

Our partner is asking now how an unwanted reality is created then if all reality is created in this space of pure Love vibration. We say to this that all reality is birthed, is manifested from vibration as you know. However, in order to create an abundant reality, one that abounds in love, peace, joy and material desires, it is centered in this space Abraham refers to as 'the vortex' for within this space, this vortex, truth is all there is. It is a pure vibrational energetic base that holds no denseness, no ego signage, no 'what-if's'; it is pure, positive vibration holding steady for you to focus upon at any given time.

The Soul & The Human Aspect

The universal love matches your vibration regardless of what that vibration is. The universal pull is a loving pull that matches, delivers, offers up, the vibration you are emitting in order to cause vibrational agreement. It's safe to put it this way for the sake of this writing: the Universe doesn't judge the vibration. There is no good or bad vibration from the Universal perspective, the perspective of the Soul. It matches the vibration because it delivers what you are asking for in the language with which it operates, and that is the language of vibration. The Universe understands how creation works and it is the intention of the Universe to create with its partners, its Soul aspects.

This is the language Cindy is speaking when we communicate with and through her. She is now able to interpret our vibration into words for the purpose of assisting in the teaching of our message. This is an inherent quality you all have. It is our intention through this series to re-introduce it to you as well for the purpose of communication with your own Soul, your own Lighthouse.

In Volume three, we gave a process for deliberate alignment that will be the first in many to come. It is a guide for the human aspect, a guideline if you will, for each individual to focus upon. You will come to realize if you haven't already, that our processes are based in freedom and that is freedom to create. We prefer labeling our processes as guidelines perhaps. They are suggested guidelines we know are subject to interpretation by each individual; they are guidelines that request input from the focus-er; input and/or intention. It is the intended action that will further the momentum toward the vibrational agreement and ultimately that forms the manifestation. Each manifestation, in whatever form, is the perfect manifestation of the vibrational agreement. In other words, it fits "to a T."

In order to create the New Earth physical reality, there are many components to be considered where the human aspect is concerned for only the human aspect is in control of its thoughts. When one proposes they have no control over their own thinking process, they have bought into the lie of powerful outside influence and control. This is never the case, for everything is controlled and moves by way of vibration. The universal eternalness is vibration and all stems from it.

In this Volume 4, we will begin to look at the expansion of the human aspect in order to create the manifestation from the available vibrational timeline that is currently at your fingertips. Never before has humanity been offered this opportunity and never before have humans experienced the vibration that is capable of creating a New Earth in the physical plane. This New Earth will be experienced individually, human aspect by human aspect, to the degree that it is focused upon which creates the momentum that will bring the physical changes into fruition. You can 'live' there at any moment you choose, and for as long as you like - vibrationally - at this point. The more who choose this experience, whether it be for a moment, an hour, a week or a year, the more intention is added to the momentum and as the momentum builds, the physical-ness will begin to show itself. It shows up in your experiences, in your government, in your schools and in your world because 'your' world is what you are creating. You experience your worlds individually and independently of each other and when the vibrations are dominant, new worlds are formed. We will get more into this concept as we move through this series.

Perhaps you've surmised by now that this series is a guideline in itself for New Earth living. We hear many of our human friends say, "there is no handbook for raising children." We'd like to propose this one moving forward. We will add suggestions for raising your children to be who they really are and how they will, automatically, shuffle in to the New Earth given the guidance to get them there. You see, they come in with all the wisdom that is available through all the strides in the expansion of consciousness you have made up to the point where they emerge. Given where they are beginning, in the midst of this New Earth vibrationally available timeline, it is they who will begin anew. It is they who will return the planet to a loving and prosperous place to live and to experience love from the Soul's perspective. And as they create, the All benefits.

So, we thank them now, as they await their perfect time of arrival to this shoreline and in the meantime, and in our own preparation, we welcome all aboard once again.

SOUL LOVE

The Soul sees no fault. The Soul never criticizes itself or another. The Soul sees Itself in everything and everyone. The Soul recognizes no mistakes. It understands vibrational choosing. The Soul only focuses on the desired experience. The Soul knows all have choice. The Soul's choice is always the expansion of Love, for it knows no other choice worthy of choosing.

The Soul loves constantly and consistently and understands all else is third dimensional illusion, readily available to Its human aspect for its choosing. The only thing ahead of you is your next choice. Choice of experience first, then the choosing of the steps of the path to get to the manifested experience. This is where the rubber meets the road so to speak. Understanding the Universal flow with which things occur is the key to happiness. It is the key to success in all areas of living in the physical plane. The key is in the choosing, and choosing love unlocks all self-constructed, illusory doors, for there is nothing that 'stands' between you and your Soul, only your belief in the illusion.

The Soul IS Love, meaning the Soul which is the God Consciousness, the Consciousness of all Love, pure Love and pure light. It cannot be anything else, for something can not be what it is not. The Soul cannot offer to another something it does not have and the Soul has no fear for fear is held in the dense vibration of the third dimension. It is defined for its human aspect by way of the ego aspect, through negative emotion, but never by the Soul.

WHAT'S LOVE GOT TO DO WITH IT?

When we told Cindy what the name of this chapter was to be, she chuckled a bit, as did we. As we've said before, we are the essence of humor, as are you. Our humor, however, can be a bit dry sometimes.

The reason we are entitling this chapter as we have is because Love has everything to do with everything. Love has been blamed for many things, is the assumed carrier of heartache on your planet and also the carrier of sheer bliss. It is when you are in this blissful state, that you are in alignment with the likes of us, your Soul.

Love is an energy. It is a vibration and it is the pure vibration of the All of everything. The denseness that you expose yourselves to is created by you and your choice of thought, you see, for when you are driving the momentum of fear, you are creating and re-creating more of the same - fear. Fear, too, is an energy and a vibration for there is nothing that is not a vibration. The fear vibration is realized through the 'mucking up' of the pure vibration, the adding of denseness where fear exists, as it were, and is the creation of the collective thinking of the human condition.

Everyone enters the earth plane as a pure vibrational being. The 'entering' we are speaking of is the conception of the human aspect in the mother's womb. The mother then, is 'responsible' for the first influence on the human that it carries. If the mother is anything other than loving during her pregnant state, the baby is influenced by the vibration that surrounds it. It all begins before there is a 'body' that you realize into. Again, every physical manifestation begins first in a vibrational state - including you.

The Soul & The Human Aspect

The love that you are, at your very core, meaning the Love that We are, is not fathomable by the human mind unless the human aspect can accept the totality of who they really are and chooses to include the influence of the Soul within their being, meaning within their thought process. As you incorporate the wisdom and knowledge of your non-physical aspect into your daily lives, you begin to understand the power that you hold within your Soul. This is one reason we are encouraging you to get in touch - be more aware of - with your Soul and to allow the larger part of you to guide you, by way of loving vibrational direction, through your physical life. The love vibration that you are contained within, is the vibration that creates worlds and is, in fact, the Universe.

This subject of Love is much bigger than we can encapsulate in one Volume so we are choosing to focus on the 'piece' or aspect of Love that concerns you, your relationships and your moving forward toward the creation of the New Earth in physical form. The acknowledgment of this aspect of Love is what is necessary, in each individual, to move the collective momentum forward toward physical realization. This aspect of Love we are speaking of is Self Love. In other words, loving you, Our human aspect, as We do.

Our human aspects get 'caught up' in what you call love in many ways and it sometimes becomes a battle ground between you. There are requirements attached to it, and rules you have ascribed to what love between two people actually means. It has become a dependency, one on another, and an efforted act that is dependent from one to another in many cases. What we mean by this is some of you believe that you cannot love another unless that one loves you, or you cannot love more than one at a time or that one must perform a list of 'acts' in order to prove love from one to another and we say to you, none of this is Love. None of these pre-conceived accolades is near the vibration of Love.

When one holds another apart from love due to jealousy, resentment and the like, this is pure indication of fear, not love. When one makes demands on another or believes another must act a certain way or 'show' proof in some way of their feeling of Love, this is not Love. This is an attempt to control another and is based in fear and insecurity. All of these illusions of the definition of Love are based in fear and stem from lack of self love for no one who understands and truly loves themselves would ask another to be anything other than who they are.

When we began our conversations with Cindy, many years ago, we began speaking of self love. Her question to us at that time was, "How do I know what it feels like if I haven't felt it before?" Since our relationship to each other is based on vibration - feeling - we had to demonstrate to her what it was by first offering a different perspective, the perspective of the Soul, of what Love was - is - for her to consider and ultimately experience through feeling. You see, as we've said many times, words do not teach. Only experience of feeling expands your wisdom of who you really are.

In order to feel something you have not experienced before, first you must believe that it is possible to experience. When one has not experienced something physically, it is impossible to liken the experience to another because all are different and when you are comparing one to another, it does not help you, you see. It creates a false-hood of experience that has the potential to lead you astray and away from the experience your Soul 'has in store' for you, its human aspect. The key to open the door to any experience you desire is first your desire and belief that it is possible for you. We say this - all experiences are possible. There is nothing you cannot be or do or have and it all begins with the vibrational asking and ends in vibrational agreement.

So, having said that, we began offering opportunities for Cindy to experience self Love through Us, you see, her non-physical aspect. This was not an easy task for her one might say, but certainly necessary for this teaching for we know and understand that many human aspects have not experienced, in their physical form, the feeling of self Love. However, you all understand and know innately, who you are and what self Love really feels like. You know this through the knowing of Us and our wisdom, you see. It is accessible for your experiencing at your request and acceptance of its validity.

When you are in-sync with your Soul's vibration, the non-physical aspect of you, you are privy to what is not readily available vibrationally in the earth plane, meaning there are simply more possibilities for understanding from Our perspective. All of these possibilities are available for your experiencing of them simply by asking, which you do every day, all day long, and then allowing for the answer to be realized by you. This is what we have referred to as 'being in the allowing state' or being in alignment.

So, in our quest for Cindy's understanding of more, we began by offering opportunities for her to trust in Us and in what we were telling her. This is the first step in your changing your belief from fear to love. There are many barriers that must be taken down in order to break through the mountains of beliefs she and many of you carry that are based in fear, about who you really are. There has been so much 'evidence' that has 'locked in' these beliefs, and from the human aspect's perspective, they are indeed 'true' so in order for you to shift and then change your perspective to include that of your Soul, you require 'evidence' of what you see as the opposite belief to be true as well.

The evidence of this current set of beliefs about who you are as unworthy and undeserving, etc., has come from many places of influence throughout your current and perhaps what you call 'past' incarnations and they stem from, generally speaking, the fears instilled and passed on to you from others. They stem from your parents, teachers, religious affiliations, those in an authoritative position and the like, and are simply beliefs that were instilled into them the same way. The momentum around the teaching of fear is strong in your current collective human vibration and in order to shift the momentum from fear to love, you must shift your perspective and conjure thoughts that will bring more love to your current vibration. This is what Abraham refers to as telling a new story.

We began offering thoughts to Cindy that would ultimately shift her perspective of her own beliefs and when she began examining them and where they came from, she quickly realized (relatively speaking) that the beliefs she had about herself were the product of the beliefs others had about themselves and she picked them up along the way in order to trust what others were telling her. Since the thoughts and words she heard from a very early age were not, in fact, in alignment with who she was - or is - they led her down the path of fear-based thinking which manifested in the belief she carried of her own unworthiness. Her story is not unlike many of our human aspects and we say this to you - you cannot be more loved for who you are, who you thought you were or who we know you will become for nothing can ultimately buck the system of love, you see. Your Soul, the expanded vibration of you who exudes pure love in every moment, is who you really are and once you begin to understand more about the aspects of you, your physical reality will shift to reflect your new beliefs about yourself.

The Soul & The Human Aspect

Love is an interesting 'concept' for the human aspect for although it is widely misunderstood, it is the only thing that has anything to do with everything. It is the healer, the peace monger and the basis to the vibrational Universe you are eternally a piece of. Your vibration reflects itself in the Universe and through you, we will create the physical New Earth however, it is your choice of when you begin to exist there. It is available to you by way of vibration and it will manifest itself to you, in your current reality by your invitation to its vibration. You invite this manifestation the way you invite all manifestation and that is through your focus upon it - your focus upon the feeling of it which is always the feeling of Love.

This feeling of Love, this vibration of Love is ever expanding and the more you focus upon those things that bring you joy and peace and are the cause of, what you refer to as, 'goose bumps', the more opportunities to experience this feeling will be brought to your forefront as you continue to choose to experience them.

As for Cindy, it took time for her to trust the likes of Us and for her to understand how this 'whole thing' works, meaning how to exist within and use the laws of the Universe to live the life she came here to experience which is one of joy, peace, love and understanding, as it is for all of you. She, like many others, had what she referred to as 'issues' with trust and of course she would have for no Love comes out of or is manifested from a basis of fear so when you (or she) is living in a fear-based existence, the momentum you are building is fear based as well. All manifestations begin in an 'out-of-alignment' state, therefore result in an 'out-of-alignment' manifestation. This is the answer to how you create an un-wanted manifestation.

It isn't until you choose to shift your perspective toward love that you allow yourself to be guided and that is when the fun begins, for you are eternal beings of light, love and mastery and when you acknowledge that and begin to trust and believe in yourself - or the Us of you - your life experience changes to reflect it and you are on a new road to discovery. This is a road that has no ending for Love is ever evolving, ever expanding and the innate vibration of You. Again, it's only ever about you for when you find your alignment, you example the truth of who you are for the All.

OUR HUMAN ASPECT

As we begin our commentary about 'you', your Soul's human aspect, we would like to say that the love we feel for you, our aspect who has wholeheartedly agreed (with joy we might add) to venture into the world of contrast, namely the earth plane, cannot be measured, nor can it be fathomed by the human mind. The love that emits through you and to you, is in actuality, your Soul loving.

All the love that any of you feel is the vibration of Us, your Soul aspect who provides love simply by Its very existence. You see, when you, the human aspect, emerges into another plane of vibration or as we've discussed in Volume 2, another vibrational timeline, you remain as the Us of you (always) yet you take on, one might say, the characteristics of that timeline. You do this by choosing the timeline as you've chosen the timeline of the third dimension.

When we say 'you take on', we don't mean to imply that anything is out of your control or that you are at the 'mercy' of any timeline you choose, you see. What we do mean is that you desire and have agreed to experience the contrasting timeline's vibration for the sole purpose of expansion; for the sole purpose of expanding your Self, which in essence means, the expansion of the Universe, beginning with You.

Our partner is asking for us to go a bit deeper here and to explain this a bit more and we say to her, our lovingly willing human aspect, to be patient and to simply allow this information to continue its own momentum and she, along with you, our reader, will understand more as we offer more understanding. Please continue.

The Soul & The Human Aspect

So, as we move forward in this description of how you, our human aspect, has chosen this particular timeline of the third dimension, you have chosen too, to be present at this timing as the Universal shift continues to evolve the earth plane to allow for more of the love vibration. As this continues to unfold, it is fueled by the dominant human collective consciousness which is evolving from the fear vibration to the love vibration that is the momentum-building factor in the creation of the New Earth in the physical plane. This is our task, our mission, our 'goal' if you will and it is yours as well, or you would not have agreed and chosen to be there at this time for you are all teachers for each other; teachers of the human aspect's evolution and you are reading this material because you have sought it out even prior to your emergence into this plane of existence. This, my friend, is part of your mission as well which is the expansion of the collective human consciousness through the expanded understanding of who you really are which is the ever-evolving vibration of pure positive energy. Simply put, the pure Christ Consciousness which is the pure light which is the purest form of Love that is ever evolving itself for the purpose of the expansion of the human Soul. This is the Oneness of the Universe and all who are willing, are playing a role - their chosen role of the expansion of themselves. But we digress.

So, as we discuss in more detail the relationship between you, our human aspect, and your non-physical aspect who is your Soul, or the 'Us' of you, we are adding to the ground work or the foundation, so to speak, of what you've already understood to be your 'Center'; that part of you Who is The 'ingredients' perhaps. This 'part' of you who, with a bit more understanding, will finally exist in your human mind as the Oneness you are attempting to experience. Let us touch on that for a moment.

THE ONENESS OF THE SOUL AND THE HUMAN ASPECT

If you've been following us for a while, you understand the concept of Oneness in that All things are a part of it. We have likened it to a puzzle, or in Cindy's analogy, the big 'pie' where all exists in its own element, being individual and All, simultaneously. We understand this is a concept that is difficult for the human aspect's mind to understand which is why you must expand your awareness to include the vibration where this concept exists. That vibration is the vibration of your Soul, or the God within you.

We have said many, many, many times that your Soul, your inner being, the God within you, is the largest part of you, meaning the most dominant vibration that is available to you at all times. In this makeup, the 'spirit' of you, which is the God vibration - your Soul, as it were - is this 'piece' that is what makes you an individual. The base, perhaps the 'bowl' of your essence is made of this vibration. It becomes unique to you as you add your own vibration, that which you conjure through the thinking of and focusing on your thoughts.

When you are in alignment with your Soul's vibration which is the steady stream that is eternally flowing and always available, you are thinking and feeling thoughts that bring you joy. These are thoughts that stem from love that carry the intention of love through to the vibration they manifest.

If you are out of alignment and choosing thoughts that are creating momentum toward fear, you are accepting thoughts that are being presented to you. This is the contrasting vibration of the third dimension. This is where our ego aspect steps in.

Every thought that has ever been thought exists in its own vibration and is there for your choosing. This includes all thought vibrations that have ever been thought that exist in fear and in love. When you are choosing love based thoughts, you are creating a momentum that will and does expand the collective vibration of love. This is how the New Earth will manifest in the physical plane - it is through the directing of your own thoughts intentionally.

However, as we've said, when you are choosing fear based thoughts, you are choosing momentum for, and simultaneously expanding, the collective fearful vibration. This is pushing against your natural state of vibratory love.

We have and will continue to discuss and suggest the acknowledgement and control of your own thinking for that is how you are creating your reality. As we move toward the expansion of the human collective love vibration, you will not only feel the shift in your own world but you will see the manifestation of it in your collective experience as well.

When we discuss Oneness, we include all things. For the purpose of our Volumed series number 4, we are including the aspects of you as well; the aspects of your Soul which is Us for Cindy and your physical ego aspect here, too. We have discussed the role the ego plays in our previous Volumes however in this portion, it becomes a more prominent aspect in the accepting of this role as part of you and part of your very Soul.

When you can acknowledge and understand you are so much more than you can see with your physical eyes and hear with your physical ears and feel with your physical bodies, you begin to understand your place within the Universe. This 'place' you hold is as a vibration that is either adding to the expansion of love or adding momentum to the vibration of fear. When you understand that your aspects, whether you can 'see' them or not, are playing their role in your experience as well, you begin to get a clue about the Oneness we speak of and the bigger role all the aspects play within it. You begin to understand your power within this Oneness and the power you have to build it or to destroy it and these actions - these behaviors - these fore-thought stepping stones are what is creating your very experience within your world.

Your Soul aspect represents for you, God. It represents All things. It exists as All things and is connected to you as part of you; as the larger part of your vibration. This vibration includes you, our human aspects. You are Us and we are You. We are connected through the love vibration that we, simultaneously, are. We are the frequency that is 'holding' you. We are the vibration you feel when you feel love, when you feel joy and when you are at peace. We are and play that role for you. We play the role of 'leader' for you in that we are where your purpose is - where the very vibration of your purpose is vibrating and calling for your focus. When you focus upon us, regardless of the 'reason' for your attention, you are adding more of our vibration to your awareness. In other words, You are expanding. It is when you 'look away' or 'ignore' or focus on the illusions that exist in the third dimension that you stumble or you 'trip' and the ego comes in to call your attention to your out of alignment choosing.

The Soul & The Human Aspect

Because you exist in a choosing based Universe, nothing is out of your control. You can choose to focus on love and you can choose to focus on fear. In either choice, there is guidance. When you choose love based thoughts, your guidance is your Soul. When you choose fear-based thoughts, your ego is your guidance. However, what has been, and is still being taught is that your ego is, for lack of a better fitting term at this time, responsible for your thinking, that the ego is responsible for all the bad thoughts in your head and that your ego is the leader in the darkness. This is never the case.

Your ego plays a similar role to your Soul in that it offers guidance through feeling. When you are feeling guidance from your Soul, you are experiencing the vibration of love and this is how you decipher that you're in alignment. When you are feeling guidance from your ego, you are experiencing the vibration of fear and this is how you decipher you are out of alignment. Neither the Soul nor the ego are choosing your thoughts. They are simply assisting you by indicating where you are vibrationally through emotional means. This is how you communicate with the All, with your spiritual 'roots' as it were, and this is through vibration. Your emotions are vibrations manifest.

Simply put, when you are in control of your thoughts, you are in control of your vibration and through your vibration you are co-creating your reality through the thought vibrations you choose to focus upon. As you focus, you expand. This is the Oneness of You. This is where your power within the Universe exists. It's all about vibration and your choosing of it. Again, simply put, your power lies within your ability to choose.

HOW THE HUMAN ASPECT WAS CREATED

As all physical manifestations, the human aspect is a conjuring of wanted experiences and the desire for more expansion. You, as the human aspect, have lived in the physical plane for many incarnations, all of which have and had a purpose. We use the word 'had' for your benefit as this is how the human who believes in 'past' lives can understand more clearly what we are saying. However, as we've stated in the previous Volumes, there is no past and no future for the future is what you are currently creating. What you refer to as 'past' lives are all happening now on alternate vibrational timelines. But we digress...

So, the human aspect was created to assist in the expansion of the All. This is why your vegetation and your animal kingdom was created as well. We understand there are many theories and many philosophies about how the human came to be however none matter at this point in your history for looking back and 'deciding' how you came to be is irrelevant to where you are heading. It is the natural process of evolution that brought you to this point, that brought your planet to this point of shifting toward a higher consciousness of pure positive love. That is where we are beginning because it matters not where you were or how you got there which, we understand, is not the way of many where 'healing' is concerned. However, we understand your whereabouts from a different perspective. When you see a rock on the ground, do you attempt to decipher where the rock came from, how it was formed and how it landed in front of you? The answer is probably not, for it matters not in that scenario, as where you are now matters not to us, it only matters that you are there.

The Soul & The Human Aspect

So, you begin to understand from the broader perspective of you that the human aspect is a 'piece' of the Soul; it is the piece of vibrational agreement who has agreed with all its aspects to venture out, as it were, to explore and experience the world of contrast on the third dimensional earth plane. The human's ability to live among the contrast comes from lifetimes of purpose and lifetimes of expansion. The degree of expansion is dependent on the choices of the human in any given physical lifetime. It is the choosing in the third plane that moves the momentum of the physical human forward, always toward its expansion of more and more love. This is and has always been the purpose, you see, which is to expand the Soul, expand the God within, for the purpose of loving more.

There are many who believe the earth will blow up or will cease in some way to exist at one time or another. We assure you this is not the case for as you understand, energy vibration cannot be destroyed. If for no other reason, this one is good enough. It is not the mindset nor is it the thought vibration that expands the human collective toward the creation of the New Earth but only adds to the momentum of the denseness that exists in your current plane. All human aspect purpose is to first and foremost expand love, you see. Even those you refer to as the 'bad' ones or the 'evil' ones who have been responsible for doing harm to his fellow man have agreed to assist in the expansion, for they provide more contrast that offers others more opportunity to choose love. This is the main focus of the human aspect as it agrees to incarnate and assist in the expansion of the Universe. It's all about the vibration of love.

Throughout history, you have asked how those of you who provide this contrast let's say, can 'go to heaven' or 'can be forgiven' for their travesties against others and we say that is a human response and an old paradigm way of thinking. We are not, in any way, advocating the disparities toward others, however we are asking you to raise your vibrational thought process to include the possibility that there might be another answer and yes, of course, there is. That answer is with us and those in the higher realms. It is not an answer that can be found amongst the denseness for the question itself is steeped in fear.

When the human aspect who appears to be 'disconnected' from its source in a way where its choosing is a product of not heeding the ego's warnings as you have seen and experienced, the manifestations that come from those choices are in line with the vibration with which they were created. These are instances where the manifestation process is clear. However, when those who appear 'connected' and are experiencing the choices of others and the effects they have on their own life experience in a personal way, this is an example of expansion, for many of you have heard us say many times when you look at something and participate in something that is not of your wanting, you are vibrationally asking for relief; you are asking for the 'solution' or the 'end' of the suffering. These requests are answered immediately and the vibration is created for the healing.

The Soul & The Human Aspect

You see, the human is living in a time-based reality where if something doesn't come to pass, one might say, or something doesn't manifest in the timeframe wanted by the human aspect, it is said to be fruitless prayer or unanswered prayer and asking. This is never the case. This too is an old paradigm way of thinking for all asking is answered. All is vibrational first. We are here to assist in the understanding of this concept, this eternal motion component for the purpose of expansion. Your asking is answered in the higher realms. It is answered vibrationally and held for you and for your timing which is event driven and that event is the alignment to your higher self, or Soul. When vibrational agreement is present, the All expands.

We will sum up this chapter of the creation of the human aspect this way and that is the laws of the Universe do not change. They are consistent and are in Universal order. Manifestation and evolution are natural processes that exist vibrationally within the universal flow, for none stand alone. The human aspect is a creation and a manifestation of vibrational agreement. The human aspect is the manifestation of love in different form and this 'form' is of your choosing. It's all of your choosing for you live in a choice-based Universe. There is not one 'thing', not one manifestation that is not chosen and all choosing - ALL choosing - is vibrational first. It is only when the agreement happens does the physical manifestation reveal itself. We say 'reveal' itself because the revelation of the physical manifestation of anything is only the 'end' result of the beginning thought and focus. It is the vibration revealed in an alternate (and physical) form.

THE INHERENT LOVE OF THE HUMAN ASPECT FOR ITS SOUL ASPECT

We begin this chapter focusing on the human aspect's non-physical form, which is Us - or your Soul. You see, and as we've said many times, the Soul is an aspect, and has many aspects. We are only beginning to introduce the 'aspects' of the Soul in this series for a broad understanding of the 'more' of you, of the vast-ness of you and your aspects. This teaching will continue to expand as the more you know of who you really are, the more momentum will be added toward the creation of the New Earth in physical form.

When the choice is made to incarnate into the third dimensional realm, that choice is made from the place - from the vibration of the most expanded awareness of you at that time which is the pure love vibration where all aspects are in alignment. The vibrational agreement, made from the place of love, carries the intention of love in with it, so to speak. The ego aspect is 'in love' and in service as is the human aspect, the now physical aspect of the consistently non-physical Soul, the aspect of God.

The 'portion' of you who journeys - vibrationally - into the third realm of existence, is what you might refer to as a 'small' part of your energy consciousness. It is the aligned focus that brings you here, simply put. It is the desire and focus of the alignment of the Soul and its aspects that manifests in the earth plane and you 'become' or re-visit your human-ness. In other words, the energy is transformed into a physical manifestation through the alignment and the focus of the aspects of you -and ta-da! Here you are.

The Soul & The Human Aspect

When you 'arrive' on the earth plane, you are a big ball of love energy. Our partner giggles when we use catch phrases and scoffs when we call them that. However, we enjoy throwing a bone once in a while...but we digress. So now, you come in as the love you are - the purest level of vibration that is 'currently' available to the All and is what makes up the All. You come in fresh and 'in love'. The love you have for your other aspects is that love that is the makeup of your Higher Self, or your Soul. It is pure and without denseness in its vibration, however taking on the physical body is the first step in its willingness to 'take on' the contrasting offerings. The physical body is the 'house' of the contrast so to speak. It is the necessary component to exist in this place of contrasting energies. Without your physical body, the experience would be in a higher realm. We are confusing Cindy a bit so let us try another angle to get this message through.

Cindy is asking how the physical body can 'house' a vibration that is not of your choosing. We like this question and will answer it this way ... the physical body does not house anything that is not of your choosing, it is a 'component' of the more dense realms of vibration, in that it is necessary for experiencing contrast; it is necessary for the 'feeling' of any contrasting vibration, you see. When we say a thought is a vibration, your body and your physical senses are what distinguish vibrations for you in the physical world. Without your body, you would not 'feel' vibration therefore you would not know when you are in or out of alignment. The Soul's vibration is 'felt' by way of loving vibrations that indicate for you that you are in alignment. The ego indicates your thought choices that are out of alignment which are also 'felt' within the body through the negative emotions. This is the makeup of your physical body and it is your feeling component to the third dimension. Simply put, it 'allows' vibrational feeling.

The inherent vibration of the human aspect is that of Love. It is the 'major' part of your eternalness and is, in effect, the vibration of the Soul and is accessible through your focus upon it. The inherent Love the human aspect has for Its Soul, or 'God' if you will, is the eternally expanding vibration that is, in any moment, the most expanded vibrational version of you. The Love that Cindy has for Us and Us for her is where our Oneness abides. It is the be all, end all to the word Love that you all express desire to 'feel'. It is there, within you in each moment and is where your power lies, not only as human aspects but as your Soul as well. This powerful vibration is the eternalness and the ever-evolving vibration of God. It is at the base of All there is and is present within every human aspect existing on the earth plane today - and always was. It simply IS.

When you feel loneliness and believe you are 'in this world' alone, this is never the case. This is only indication that your focus is on something that is not real and is directed outside of your Self; you are out of alignment with your Soul for you are never, never are you, separate from God - your Soul or your Higher Self - this is the illusion of the third dimensional realm and is steeped in fear. It is the most fear-based thinking in your world today and is where all the chaos stems from, you see. When all are of the understanding of their own aspects and the power you hold within them to simply love, the New Earth will manifest from this ongoing momentum. Your collective focus will make it so. It cannot be another way for you are loved beyond your own comprehension and until this note is recognized, acknowledged and lived, you will continue to thrive in the third dimensional realm of your reality. It is love that will heal your world and it all begins with your acknowledging of that statement. Love Heals and you are Love. It is the natural make-up of your eternal Soul.

YOUR SOUL IS THE EXPANDED VERSION OF YOU, ITS HUMAN ASPECT

As you know by now, we are revealing more and more of who you really are to you for the purpose of expansion. We, as the collective consciousness and non-physical aspect of Cindy, or her Soul as it were, are the expanded vibrational version of her. This means we are existing as the vibration she has expanded to through her desire for expansion. Yes, this is a collective desire of course, and is how the Universe expands itself, through all Its aspects and their individual and simultaneous expansion.

Before her incarnation into the earth's vibrational timeline, there was vibrational agreement with all the aspects of Cindy, which includes the physical aspect that she represents, her non-physical and 'higher vibrational' aspect, which is Us, and many aspects she has lived, all existing on their own vibrational timeline. We know this is what you might call a deep subject, however it will open you up to your own expansion with your understanding of it.

As we described in our previous Volumes, there are many aspects that make up the One who you call God. These aspects, these vibratory patterns or vibrational timelines, consist of all the thought vibrations that ever existed. As you move through your physical life, you are adding to the momentum of these other timelines as you re-visit or choose thought patterns from them. When you make those choices, you add to and agree with these vibrations and you create or re-create, in physical form, the manifestations of those thought choices.

The Soul & The Human Aspect

When you choose to allow your Soul to guide you, you are 'taking advantage of' the expanded knowing you have 'acquired', so to speak. This 'knowing' is vibrational. This space is what Abraham refers to as your Vortex. This is the space - the vibrational timeline - where all your desires are waiting for you; the matching vibration is there, holding the space for you. When you allow yourself to 'go with the flow' and to move on impulse, impulses from your Source, your Soul, you move beyond what you refer to as 'blocks'. These 'blocks', in essence, are simply vibrational patterns that are of the vibrational timeline you are currently visiting and those vibrational patterns cannot exist on the new timeline you are moving toward. Let us simplify this concept for you.

As your Soul aspect, we emit the expanded vibrational pattern of the human aspect - and all the aspects of your Soul. This vibration is the expanded version of who you refer to as God. It is the vibration of the All and exists without denseness. It contains and is made up of all the love vibrations you have added through your eternal life experience, whether it be physical or non-physical. In other words, it is the most evolved version of You - and it is vibrational.

You, as our Human Aspect, have access to this vibration for it is your desire to vibrate as your natural state of being. This is the desire for alignment. As you live your life experience in the earth plane, you are met with choices in each moment. The choices you make, in each moment, are the key to your own creation, the creation of your own reality. Your power lies within your choosing of vibration and you choose your vibration by choosing your thoughts and assigning them meaning.

As you expand your awareness of who you really are, you are met with more choices and these choices are 'new' to you as they are choices that are presented from the new timeline vibration that you are expanding 'into' or 'onto' if you prefer.

As you allow your Soul to lead and guide you forward, the fear some of you experience is the fear of this unknown vibrational pattern and the choices that are now in front of you. This fear, of course, is an illusion and is constructed by you and your choosing of more comfortable thoughts, thoughts that you can and have controlled the outcome of. In other words, in your mind, your control sits with what you have experienced and not where you have no experience - yet. However, the opposite is also true.

When you are allowing your Soul to lead you to the expanded version of you, to the new timeline as it were, the control you have is for your motion forward; the control you have is in the choosing to trust your Source, your Soul, for the guidance that is necessary for your expansion. You see, this expanded version of you, or your Soul, already knows where you are coming to. It is there and coaxing you toward the desires that you hold, not the least of which is the expansion of love. It is, simply put, God calling you forward toward peace, joy and abundance. You choose to trust your own human knowing or you choose to trust the Source of All, your Soul, or God. You hold within this choice, your own expansion.

THE SOUL'S LOVE FOR THE HUMAN ASPECT, EXTENDED THROUGH ITS EGO ASPECT

If you've been reading our work, you are of the understanding that the ego of you, the third dimensional traveler who assists in your experience in the earth plane, is there, by your side, for one reason and that is to present choice - for you.

When you live in a contrasting space with unlimited thought vibrations from which to choose, the ego, in a nutshell, indicates to you, by way of negative emotion, the choices you have made that are not in alignment with those thoughts of love from the Soul. The ego, or the Soul for that matter, however is not the 'chooser' of your thoughts. Nothing, no thought or choice, is ever 'infused' or forced 'into' you. This is a misaligned teaching, as it is fear-based thinking at its base.

You see, every thought vibration that has ever been thought still exists. No vibration 'goes away' although it may lay dormant when not focused upon. All thoughts are available to you for your choosing. When you choose thought vibrations of love, peace, joy and the like, these are offered for your consideration from your Soul aspect. When you choose thought vibrations that are not offered by your Soul, your ego simply steps in to bring it to your attention. The way it gets your attention is through the negative emotions and feelings based in fear. This is the clear distinction that the ego provides for you and that is to simply choose again and choose yourself back into alignment with your Soul's guidance.

The Soul & The Human Aspect

You see, you cannot feel negative emotion of any kind when you are in alignment. Therefore, you would not know you are out of alignment unless another part of you - in this case, your ego - was to make you aware of the momentum you are building in the opposite direction from your Soul. It is imperative to the expansion of the human collective that all shift the perspective of the current understanding of the ego as a fear-based entity to one of love and one who is the assistant to its human aspect, standing in service to the Soul.

All aspects of the Soul are loved unconditionally and the ego is one of your aspects. The love of the Soul is 'extended' you might say, to the human aspect in the third dimension through the likes of the ego. As the Soul does not 'play' in the lower vibrations, the ego is there, playing with you, its human aspect, as a 'stand in' one might say, to its Soul aspect. You are all a 'team' that works in tandem in order to expand love.

The Soul provides the stream of the love vibration and indicates to you and for you by way of positive emotions; by way of love, peace and joy and when you are feeling and experiencing any of these emotions, you are in alignment with the thought vibrations of the Soul. On the other hand, when the human aspect is 'confused' or caught up in the chaos that is available to participate in, the ego stands in service to not only the Soul but to the human aspect as well, through love. You see, you are One with all and this Oneness includes your ego aspect.

The Soul - God - loves all, including the ego which is meant to assist the human aspect. The ego has agreed to protect, in a sense, and to offer guidance from the contrasting side of the earth's third dimensional realm for the sole purpose of presenting choice to the human aspect. As the earth ascends, as it is now, it offers the opportunity for all its inhabitants to ascend as well and as this happens, the 'light' gets 'lighter' and the denseness gets more dense. Without the assistance of the ego in this realm, the human aspect who is not acknowledging who it really is, can easily be swayed we would say, or influenced more and more into the denseness. The ego 'throws the rope' by way of indicating the denseness in your thought choice that is present. This 'rope' as it were, is the stream of negative emotion. By offering this rope to you - this feeling of separation - it offers the human aspect an 'out', so to speak. It offers the human aspect of itself the way to choose love once again and this is done by pointing out the contrast that is offering the choice.

We have said many times in many ways that the ego is not the thinker of the negative thoughts nor is it the 'one in your mind' who is causing the chaos. This is a wide misunderstanding of what and who the ego is and the role it plays for you through the love of the Soul. Every thought that has ever been thought is a vibration and is available for your choosing.

We have offered this visual to Cindy on many occasions to example what it may be like for the human aspect and the control you have of the choosing of your thoughts. The visual is one that takes you to the side of a creek or a small river, happily flowing on its own. As you sit on the river bank, you see 'thoughts' flowing by you, all for your choosing. Cindy pictures them as flowers of different colors, those of the Soul are white and those not of the Soul's choosing are shades of darkness. It is her choice to pluck them out of the river as she chooses the experience they will then manifest.

The Soul & The Human Aspect

As you are sifting and choosing your thoughts from the vast limitless river that is surrounding you every day, you are in control of the 'consequences' those thoughts will bring - yes, please change 'consequences' to manifestations as 'consequences' implies hardship to many - and this, our dear friend, is how you are creating your reality. You are choosing your vibrational manifestations first by choosing your thoughts, then you are assigning to them a meaning. From that meaning, you create.

Now perhaps you have a different and more loving perspective of the role your ego plays within your life experience for the love of the Soul exists in the ego as well and if you shift your perspective from fear to love regarding your thoughts of the ego, you will expand (or raise) your vibratory pattern and enhance your experience in the third dimensional realm. All of this comes from the love the Soul has for all its aspects, none more important or loved more than another, for you are One with your Soul and One with your ego and the love in this collective vibration abounds.

HOW THE HUMAN ASPECT FITS INTO THE PROCESS OF EVOLUTION

The reason we are revealing who we are, in regards to Seth and Abraham, is to demonstrate the process of conscious evolution in terms the human aspect can understand, and it helps some who can visualize its movement better as a process unfolding, as Cindy does. It is helpful in some regards simply because evolution is, what you might call, a 'big' concept, and one that is not easily fathomed by the human mind that 'instills' limits on itself because of the contrast it is surrounded by. The contrast is noticeable to the degree you choose to notice it. On the other hand, it is your focus upon it that creates the degree of notice-ability, you see, as in all things. The more aware you become of your ability to choose and create your own reality, the choice is yours to continue to bask in the contrast or in your choosing to move beyond it. This choice is what will create the New Earth in physical form.

When we began revealing ourselves - the 'state' of ourselves that is - as the evolutionary vibration of Seth and Abraham to Cindy, (that is not to say the consciousness that we are - that you are - that the All is - is not available to anyone who focuses upon it. The names we choose are for teaching and exampling purposes only, and are necessary for most in the third dimensional plane) we offered her a visual she could relate to. Our visual was likened to a propeller plane pulling signs through the air while one is visiting a beach resort of some kind. As the plane moves slowly through the sky above, you are drawn to reading the signage and advertisements for some message that is meant to be conveyed. In our case, we wanted Cindy to understand in one moment who we were 'following' and she instantly knew who we were and what the base of our message is, and that is one of expansion of the Universal Love Vibration.

The Soul & The Human Aspect

There are many who are communicating with their non-physical aspects knowingly however most are still living by default. You are always in your perfect 'spot' of your own evolution and your evolution is not something you can 'rush' to - or through - for it is a never-ending process and the process itself is eternal evolution.

Cindy is asking now if we, her Soul (and yours), continue to evolve when there is not contrast and we say of course, for evolution is an ever changing, consistent motion forward. As you, our human aspects experience and evolve within the physical world, the All evolves right along with you. This is how the Universe expands for nothing 'sits still' but is in constant motion. We are vibration, the Universe is vibrationally based, pure and simple. Vibration, if it were to 'stop', would not be 'moving'; your own definition of 'vibrate' is 'to move or cause to move consistently.' You are, in essence, always 'alive' for your alive-ness is the vibration of you, you see.

Let us back up for a moment on this subject of vibration and how we, as your non-physical vibration, 'live' and expand through and by the likes of you, our human aspect. You see, when you - 'we' collectively - agree to experience the earth plane of contrasting vibrations, our intention is to expand through the choosing of a more expanded vibration of who we are which is the pure vibration of love. We (all) expand each time you choose love, or choose to 'be' who you really are which is 'us' in your pure vibratory state. We understand this can be a bit confusing so let us give you an analogy with which to clear it up.

Let us say you are standing in wait for a subway car. You are surrounded by others who are waiting for the same car, moving in the same direction. As you step on the car to, in essence, move forward in your physical journey, all others step on too, all moving in the same direction. As this analogy may seem a little 'off beat' to you, it is the demonstration of your choice - and the others' choice - to move forward. It is simultaneous motion, all participators - or in our case, all aspects - moving forward with the same intention, all in the same direction.

We, as the 'larger part of you', being your non-physical aspect, are a combination of not only All that is, but All of our collective timelines as well. The role you are currently playing, the human aspect role, has access to all these vibrational timelines as well because you are One with us. When the human aspect 'steps out' to experience the contrast that will manifest a broader perspective of 'itself' by way of expanding the pure vibration of love, Us, as it were - it takes on the experience, knowing and choosing it from the basis of the broader perspective of who it is, with the desire to expand for the good of All. This is the overall intention of the Universal vibration and one purpose (and there are many) for the Universal Law of Attraction. It serves Us well, for the good of all, by the consistent delivery of the matching vibration of all desires held by not only the human collective, but all vibrational desires put forth 'into' the Universal field of vibration. But we digress...

The Soul & The Human Aspect

The human aspect's role, its overall intention in its choosing to experience the physical realm, is first and foremost, expansion of the All. You see, when you are in your non-physical state, blended with the larger vibrational part of you - who is the 'Us' of you - you see from the broader perspective and you understand fully who you are in the whole scheme of things. This perspective is then 'limited' by the third dimensional realm due to the contrasting vibrations offered for consideration. This is a known element to the non-physical part of you, however the ego's assistance is also 'known' and the aspects, in essence, take the trip together in order to accomplish the intention of expansion.

The role you play, as the human aspect of the Soul, is as important as all your other aspects, not one better or more important than another for one cannot exist without the other and therein lies the key to your sense of your own worthiness for you are the God you believe you are 'praying' to and the 'God' vibration is the larger part of who you really are. The importance of the human aspect to the overall expansion of the Universe cannot be understood by most who make up the human collective consciousness at this time and is the reason we are here to assist in your knowing of who you really are.

We encourage you to seek more about yourself through this and other teachings that resonate with you, and to understand more about your innate power within the Universe you contributed to - that you contribute to in each moment through the inherent vibration that you hold. It is imperative to the evolution of not only your planet and in the creation of your New Earth, but also to the expansion of All that is. It IS that big.

ALIGNMENT

All those who choose to 'channel consciousness' for others, make a decision to be outwardly criticized, to one degree or another, by your current societal "standards". By most 'onlookers' in the beginning, less as the journey continues, and usually respected at the end of the run, so to speak. This is an avenue of clear and deliberate choosing and once it begins, it expands quickly (relatively speaking.) The vast majority who decide to live 'as', example, and teach 'spirituality' for lack of a better word, never return fully to the third dimensional way of life - or better said, they expand beyond the core denseness and their physical reality morphs into the new reality, constructed by dominating thoughts of love. In other words, they live the example they teach. It is, of course, inevitable.

This examples our teaching that states, "you cannot go back" - you cannot 'un-vibrate'. So, your spiritual community is exampling and living the laws of the Universe, all evolving at their own pace and teaching as they 'remember' - and mostly by example. Teaching one thing and living another is the nemesis of the process.

The first 'live' channeling gathering Cindy held was made up of 10 people. She knew them and they were there not only to experience communication with another dimension (and in reality, another aspect of themselves) but to support her in this 'new endeavor' she had decided to embark on with Us, the non-physical aspect of herself. Cindy is commenting about our use of your language and she'd like for us to say it in a different way; a way that may be more 'real' to those who are reading this. We will indulge her and restate our words this way ... "she was doing something weird that most of them had not witnessed before and they wanted to see if it might be true." At the end of the session, let's just say, they felt the vibration of truth and it resonated. Every one of them left the gathering with a different perspective of a belief they carried.

The reason we are telling this story of the first channeling session for Cindy is because of the first question she received during that demonstration of one who is allowing and communicating with her own Soul guidance. The question was, 'How do we get into alignment? How do we do what Cindy is doing?"

We have been teaching for years, "words do not teach." You are exampling that truth each day you experience something that shifts your perspective from what you thought it should be to what it turned out to be, by way of your experiencing of it. Regardless of what "it" is. It matters not. This is how shift happens. It is by way of and through the living of experiences. Some you enjoy, some you don't. As you begin to sift and syphon through what thoughts are manifesting what, you begin to focus on your choice of thought and you realize, in the physical sense, how you are creating what you are living. Then you begin to tweak it and soon you are pre-paving your next moment by loving in the moment before it - and by this, and through love, you expand. This is the process of moving into alignment by choosing those thoughts that feel good - thoughts based in love, offered by your Soul. It begins with understanding who you really are.

This is an important teaching for New Earth living. New earth living IS consistent pre-paving however, the pavers are blocks of love, one right after another. So you're not only creating consciously by your thoughts, but you are enjoying the manifesting of those thoughts at the same time since you are manifesting your desired experiences. This is New Earth living. You see, when one is in this state - a steady state of alignment, there is only love.

It's not an easy thing to do, to live in consistent alignment within the earth plane's contrast however, it is the 'event' if you will, that will take you to the next step of expansion which is, for the collective human consciousness, the creation of the new human aspect and simultaneously, the creation of the New Earth in physical form. The 'event' that takes place on an individual level first, is the releasing of the denseness you are choosing moment by moment, for as each individual chooses love in each moment, the expansion of their individual spirit - awareness - vibration causes the simultaneous expansion of the human collective and ultimately (and simultaneously) the Universe as a whole. This is the process of evolution you are contributing to vibrationally.

Expansion is a vibrational process and is within your control as is your choosing of alignment. As you choose love in each moment, you are deliberately creating momentum toward your own alignment. As you continue to focus upon love instead of fear, you spend more and more 'time' in alignment with who you really are. One by one, you will create the momentum that will dominate the collective consciousness of humanity. This will result in the physical manifestation of the vibration that is existing now which is the vibration of the New Earth.

OUR PARTING WORDS

We are grateful you are traveling this journey with us and are focused on your own evolution, while we all make our way to the physical manifestation of the New Earth. This is indeed an exciting time for all of humanity and for your Soul brethren as well, for as you embark on this creation with the Universe, it is this time, in your time space reality, that is the first of many opportunities that are before you.

As we've said, as you expand your own awareness - your own vibration - to include the higher realms of your multi-dimensional selves, you are privy to and have opportunities to choose those possibilities that exist within those more expanded vibratory patterns. In other words, the further 'out' you go, the 'more' there is to choose from. Yes, you can picture it as Cindy is visualizing it in this moment and that is the difference between walking in to a small convenience store and walking into your Walmart. There are simply more options from which to choose your experiences.

As we move forward in our continued teaching of who you really are, we will encompass all that we have already spoken of and what you will experience is a 'coming together' of sorts; the information, when accumulated to the degree of dominance, meaning when the information we are offering is accepted, acknowledged and combined within your current vibration, you will feel shift after shift after shift for when the perspective of the Soul is 'put into action' so to speak, you will experience your physical reality reflecting those shifts. In other words, you will be manifesting the vibration you hold as you are now, and always do.

We encourage your continued motion forward in whatever way you choose, knowing in each moment more and more of who you are, and as you include more of Us, more of the vibration of your Soul into your own awareness, you will continually and naturally seek more.

This is a never-ending journey for it is the journey of your very Soul and through this work and any teaching that resonates with you, you are consciously participating in your own Soul's evolution. As you 'add to your repertoire', vibrational repertoire that is, you will naturally be drawn to more. This is what the Soul journey is about at its core vibration and that is to expand and experience the love that It, Itself, is for nothing is more pleasing to the Soul than Love, for from the Soul's perspective, there is only Love for Love lovingly Rules the Universe and the human aspect is moving toward this understanding more and more every day. The more of you, our beloved human aspects, who choose Love in each turn, will experience the evolution of your Soul and will, at long last, experience Oneness with Everything.

We wish you well on your journey and we instill in you, from our vibration to yours, a love you have not experienced yet for New Earth vibration is the most expanded version of You that has ever existed.

Revel in the new You, go forth and Live It.

We are Josef.

Quotes & Commentary
By Josef...

Your Soul, You,
The Human Aspect Of Your Soul,
And Your Ego,
The Ego Aspect Of Your Soul,
Choose To Play Together
In The 3rd Dimension
For One Overall Purpose
And That Is
So All Aspects Of Your Soul
- All Aspects Of God -
Can Co-Create
An Expanded Version
Of Themselves.
When All Aspects
Are Co-Creating
You Are In Alignment.

The Soul & The Human Aspect

In a nutshell...

As we focus upon the three aspects that are prevalent within the third dimensional realm, your Soul, your ego and you, our collective human aspect, we understand how they work in tandem to create more of themselves, which is the All. This means they all play their individual and collective roles in the co-creation of the expansion of God, the expansion of the Universe.

When you are playing nicely together (so to speak) in the third dimension, you, the human aspect, is being guided toward your purpose and desires by your Soul, the 'Us' of Cindy. As you are sorting and sifting your way through the contrasting atmosphere in your earth plane, you are bumping up against contrasting vibrations that may throw you off course and therefore out of alignment with your Soul. This is where your loving ego steps in to assist.

When all three aspects are 'in sync', the human aspect is aware of its guidance from the Soul, the larger part of its vibration and also aware of the role the ego plays in keeping it in alignment with the Soul's intention of love by indicating its vicinity to alignment by way of negative emotion. Both the Soul and the ego are communicating with the human aspect through emotional means. The Soul offers validation through good-feeling emotion meaning when you are choosing loving, peaceful, joyful thoughts, you are manifesting the matching vibrations and it is from these vibrations that you are creating.

On the other hand, when you are being influenced out of alignment and are choosing negative vibrational thoughts, your ego points this out to you through negative emotion. This is your indication that you have focused away from the thoughts of your Soul, the thoughts your Soul offers about the subject or situation at hand. These signs are what Cindy refers to as the ego's warning signs that are, in essence, telling you through negative emotion, to re-focus or as Abraham says, 'return to the highlighted route."

It is when these three aspects of your Soul are working together that you are in the allowing state of expansion. Within this expansion, are the vibratory matches to all you desire. It is this vibration, the pure vibration of the Soul, that is the pure vibration of God and this is what we refer to as 'being in the vortex." This, our dear friend, is your point of creation. You choose your way 'in' based on how you feel at any given moment.

The Feeling Of Love Is The Manifestation Of The Vibration Of The Soul.

The Soul & The Human Aspect

In a nutshell...

As you understand, all vibration manifests as you focus upon it. When you, the human aspect, feel love, you are focused on the vibration of love, which emanates from your Soul and your 'feeling' of love, in all its expressions, are the physical manifestation of the pure vibration of your Soul.

As we taught in our previous Volumes, all love, all experiences of love whether they be romantically focused, a focus upon a child, pet or nature for that matter, are centered in and delivered to you emotionally through the vibration of your Soul. It, the vibration of the Soul, expresses itself and validates for you, its human aspect, your Oneness with yourself; it is the exampling of your Oneness with your Soul aspect and also with your ego aspect in that when you are in alignment with your Soul, it is also indication you are in alignment with the true desire of your ego as well, which is your alignment with you Soul. When you are in alignment, you feel no contrasting emotion.

All expressions of love are manifestations of your Soul's vibration or the vibration of God, if you prefer. Love is felt and expressed. It is not an action for it is who you really are. In other words, a spoon does not require action to be what it is. It provides a service and in our case, in the case of love, the 'service' love provides is the expansion of itself.

Love is the eternal nature of the Universe and its purpose is to expand itself for all to experience. Each time any aspect of the Universe experiences the love vibration, it expands itself for although there are many, limitless in fact, expressions and experiences of love, no two are the same. This is the uniqueness that you are. It is the uniqueness and sameness of your Soul which is your connection to all that is. It is what is known as the Universal mystery in your world. To Us, the God of you, the Universe in all its glory, it is The Way. All there really is, is Love. We suggest you revel in it as often as you can understand that your reveling is what is creating the more of you and the more you revel, the more you add to the loving vibration of the Universe. It is, after all, your consistent contribution to what some of you refer to as God.

When You Are In Alignment
With Your Soul, All Possibilities
For Manifestation Are Available
To You By Way Of Your Soul's Current
Vibration, Which Is
Your Non-Physical Aspect.
As You Experience This More
Expanded View Of Yourself,
You Become Aware Of
The Possibilities For Manifestation In
This Expanded Space.
This Is The Beginning Stage
Of Co-Creation Where We Supply
The Vibratory Pattern First,
And You Expand Your Vibration
To Receive It.
This Is The Co-Creation
Of Vibrational Agreement.

The Soul & The Human Aspect

In a nutshell...

All manifestations begin in the vibratory state first. This is how what you ask for is indeed 'given'. When you desire something, you are asking the Universe vibrationally. The Universe does not 'hear' your words for many times what you say and what you 'vibrate' are in contrast.

The Universe and all aspects of you - including the You of Us - communicate through vibration. Vibration is the language with which your Soul and ego communicate with you and these vibrations, or this vibrational language rather, manifests itself emotionally within the human aspect. So it stands to reason that this is, too, how you communicate with Us and the Universe as well. Vibration is the Universal language as gravity is a Universal 'law'. You refer to them as Universal Laws. We prefer Universal Experiences.

To achieve vibrational agreement and to experience the manifestation of your desires, the human aspect must experience the matching vibration, through physical means, which is the vibration that We hold or that is held by the Universe, which is the vibration that is given that matches the asking vibration you have put forth. In other words, it is the two pieces of the magnet coming together to create the 'snap'. It is a manifestation that happens within the 'magnetic field'.

When you 'ask', we offer the vibration that matches the pure vibration of what you're asking for. We don't deal is resistance, you see. This 'matching vibration' will hold steady, throughout eternity if necessary, until you, the physical component, offer the matching vibration which creates the physical manifestation. You see, in order to bring something into the physical plane, the physical aspect (you) must match the non-physical aspect's offering, which is the offering of the Soul. When the human aspect releases the resistance from within that vibration, the manifestation appears. This is co-creation at its best. This is an example of the knowing of who you really are and the power that you hold within your ability to choose. You choose your way to alignment by releasing the illusory resistance held within the third dimensional realm. By continuing to release the resistance to your Soul's vibration, your physical vibration expands.

The human collective has been asking for a New Earth for quite some time. This asking comes by way of the contrast in which you live. Each time an individual 'asks' for better circumstances, in any situation, the Universe holds the vibration of pure love for it is in asking from compassion that the New Earth will manifest. It is in the asking for help and assistance from your Souls and this help comes through many means, all steeped in Love and manifesting in the revealing of more of who you are.

You are in the process of the creation of many things, not the least of which is the New Earth and all the components that go with it. We offer you guidance toward more of the loving vibration for that is where all possibilities exist, all based in and made of pure positive love. Love, in its pure essence, is at the base of all vibrational agreement for when you, our physical aspect and We, your non-physical aspect are in alignment, all things are possible.

Your Soul's Vibration Is Where Love Emanates From. This Love Is The Feeling Of Alignment, Manifest In You, Your Soul's Human Aspect.

The Soul & The Human Aspect

In a nutshell...

As you now understand our perspective, the perspective of your Soul, and that all love that exists everywhere emanates from your Soul vibration, and that all the aspects of your Soul are 'born' from this love vibration, you understand that you, our beloved human aspect are born from love as well. All aspects of what you refer to as God are based in love therefore are love at the core of their existence.

All things that are born of or emanate from any vibration contain within them the vibration of that desired emergence, so to speak, therefore manifest from that vibration as well. You are the physical manifestation of the loving vibration of your Soul, brought forth through the desire to co-create in the earth plane.

Your Soul's vibration is the dominant vibration of your makeup. This cannot be changed but can be thwarted by you in your choosing of experiences. As you experience your physical life in the third dimensional realm, you are offered all experiences from which to choose from the 'bag' of vibrations available to you at any time. In order to remain in alignment with your Soul, the key is to choose from the 'bag' of loving vibrations that will manifest in loving experiences regardless of the desire at hand.

When you feel good - when you are feeling love, joy, peace or abundance, your Soul is indicating to you through emotional means. These emotions are the communication between your Soul and its aspects, you see. All emotional experiences are indications of your alignment with your Soul.

The love of the Soul is always available for your choosing. It is your most natural state of being and your vibrational communication is what allows you to remain in 'contact' with your Soul and the other aspects of you. It is the desire of all the Soul aspects to remain in alignment because all aspects come forth, throughout eternity, to expand the love that they are, the love that is and emanates from your Soul. This is the co-creation of the evolution of the Universe and comes by way of vibrational agreement with the pure vibration of love of the Soul.

**Always
Look
Toward
The Love
In All
Situations,
Not
At The Fear.**

The Soul & The Human Aspect

In a nutshell...

The love of the Soul is always available to you as the beam of light from a lighthouse in a storm. It is there as your guidance, your way to safety, some might say. This beam of light is the loving vibration of your Soul. Regardless of where you may be vibrating in any given moment, this vibration is part of who you are. It is available for you to 'tap into' any time you choose.

Anything you focus upon gets bigger. We have been teaching this energetic concept for many eons. As you focus, the vibration with which you focus, expands. This is evident within your societal issues. As the dominant human collective vibration is focused upon any issue, stating the desire to be one of ridding your world of such atrocities, the 'issue' at hand expands in your awareness. As this happens, the dominant vibration, in essence, 'fights' back by adding more focus upon it. It demonstrates itself for you by way of the manifestation of more of the same.

We suggest the handling of these 'issues' in a different way, the exact opposite way in fact, and that is to focus on the love vibration within the issue instead of the fearful vibration that continues to increase the size of the issue. Since everything you focus upon expands, by focusing on the love, you will then manifest a more loving way with which to solve your 'issues'.

You see, as you focus upon the fearful vibrations of any issue, you are focused upon the problem that created them. By focusing on the love vibration, you are focused on the solution, which is always available for your choosing. However, the solution is born of love, not fear. It matters not how much fear you pour onto an issue in the hopes of resolution, you simply can't get to any solution by way of fear. Some have said, "you cannot solve a problem with the same (vibration) that created it." We've altered this a bit for our purposes but the concept is certainly correct. When you are reaching for resolution, reach for and focus upon love. All manifestations of the loving vibration of the Soul are loving manifestations as well. It's all about vibrational agreement. If you are offering a fearful vibration about anything, you will manifest more fear. It really is that simple.

Procrastination Is Indication Of Skewed Alignment. Simply Put, It's Just Not Time Yet.

The Soul & The Human Aspect

In a nutshell...

We feel our human friends, many of you in fact, claim to be procrastinators and think that is a 'bad' thing. In some cases, perhaps it is based on your human reasoning for not moving forward or not taking action that you believe will put you in the place you want to be with any project, task or undertaking. We offer this perspective to all who claim to be procrastinators in the hope it may alleviate some undesired pressure you impose on yourselves around this subject.

In vibrational terms and from our perspective, procrastination is one of the ego's emotional flags, telling you that you are out of alignment just as any negative emotion indicates. This unbalanced state, this vibrationally vulnerable state rather, is the cause of the procrastination. It is the reason for the unsettled feeling about the subject at hand.

We offer you this where procrastination is concerned - when you are wavering, when you are out of alignment, you are making choices and decisions of action that are too out of alignment with what your Soul is 'holding' vibrationally for you, which is what you asked for, in its most expanded form. The feeling of procrastination in this case is a feeling of 'fear' in that you 'think' you should do something but you cannot 'bring' yourself to do it for whatever reason. You are intentionally distracting yourself from the action simply because your Soul's guidance is telling you it is not time yet to make the move. When it is time, there is no feeling of, what Cindy refers to as, angst.

On one hand, it is never, never is it beneficial to you to take action when you are out of alignment for all steps that will come from this beginning position are, too, out of alignment, therefore the manifestation will be out of alignment as well. In this case, your Soul's guidance, in a sense, is distracting you from taking the next step because by your knowing what this 'discord' means, you can feel, for yourself, you are not in alignment with your own desire. In other words, the procrastination is a way of moving past the fear and allowing the Soul to guide you toward the logical next step, that will be in alignment and will lead you to your in-alignment manifestation. When you are listening to your ego's prodding, the message is always that you are out-of-alignment.

We would put the word 'procrastination' in your bag of goodies you carry around that holds the knowing you have about where you sit vibrationally where your alignment with your Soul is concerned. When you are feeling procrastination, you now understand that you are hesitating for a reason and this reason is you are not in alignment and there is something better for you beyond this step you are contemplating. When you acknowledge this knowing, and relax and allow your Soul to guide you, the logical next step or steps will be presented to you at the perfect time. This is event driven manifestation where your Soul is guiding you, step by step vibrationally, toward your in-alignment manifestations. Procrastination is just another opportunity for choosing trust for when the way is made clear, you will know it and hesitation will not be part of your equation. Trust your Soul's knowing and focus on your alignment. This is the path of least resistance.

Now,
Go Love Yourself
As We Do.

The Soul & The Human Aspect

In a nutshell...

The love that we share, the Oneness that we share, your Soul, your aspects and You, is not describable in human words. It is a feeling that is beyond your comprehension so much so that if you were to acknowledge it and allow yourself to feel the fullness of it, the fullness of who you really are that is, there would be peace among you.

This vibration that we are, and that you are at your very core, is at the bottom of every loving manifestation that ever was and that will ever be. It is the vibration of the most expanded version for the Universe and Its laws that assist in the evolving creation of Itself - and it is powerful. This vibration, this love vibration is where your power comes from and where the power in All emanates from and that is the Power of Love.

When you allow your Soul to lead you, eventually, when there is no resistance left within you, you will feel it for yourself. This, our dear friend, is the love that is the truth that sets you free.

Printed in Great Britain
by Amazon